The Little Book of
ZLATAN

MALCOLM OLIVERS

HarperCollins*Publishers*

HarperCollins*Publishers*
1 London Bridge Street
London SE1 9GF

www.harpercollins.co.uk

First published by HarperCollins*Publishers* 2017

1 3 5 7 9 10 8 6 4 2

© Malcolm Olivers 2017

Malcolm Olivers asserts the moral right to
be identified as the author of this work

A catalogue record of this book is
available from the British Library

ISBN 978-0-00-826350-8

Printed and bound in Germany by
GGP Media GmbH, Pößneck

MIX
Paper from
responsible sources
FSC™ C007454

This book is produced from independently certified FSC™ paper
to ensure responsible forest management

For more information visit: www.harpercollins.co.uk/green

CONTENTS

AN UNEXPECTEDLY SERIOUS INTRODUCTION

Throughout history, there have been many, many truly outstanding sportsmen and women. These are the individuals who have pushed the boundaries of their sport, set incredible new records or driven the human body to its physiological limits. Every day we celebrate the feats of the fastest, strongest and most brilliantly technical athletes on the planet.

However, if we interrogate that history further, there are some individuals who stand head and shoulders above the others, modern-day heroes who can be given the status of 'icon' or 'legend' and who are consequently bequeathed a peerless position in society and memory. These individuals are not only differentiated by their awe-inspiring dominance of their own sport but by the way in which we – the normal folk – reflect upon their contribution and indeed their cultural legacy.

What makes Muhammad Ali, Ayrton Senna, Usain Bolt and Maradona the greatest of all time? Is it the success they achieved or the way in which they achieved it?

As an obsessive fan of Zlatan Ibrahimović it can be easy to descend into hyperbole, and clearly it may be a step too far to put him on a pedestal with some of the greats above. In fact, it might be argued that, in the era of Lionel Messi and Cristiano Ronaldo, Zlatan cannot even be compared to his brilliantly gifted footballing contemporaries, let alone the most legendary athletes of all time.

So why write a book entirely dedicated to the third best player on the planet? Why celebrate a man who is renowned for his volatility as much as his extraordinary aerial prowess?

The answer – perhaps reassuringly in an era of big data, football academies and sports science – lies in the cult of personality. Zlatan is an icon not just because of his extraordinary records on the field, but because his *personality* has never had to take a back seat on the journey. Would Zlatan be a good guest at a party? *The answer is yes, of course!* Would Zlatan make a good big brother? *Definitely.* Would Zlatan have been successful if he had chosen a different career path, perhaps as a teacher, a builder or a karate coach? *There is a very good chance he would have excelled in all three – all at once . . .*

Zlatan Ibrahimović has an undeniable gravitas and charisma that makes us want to follow him on and off the field. He has a mercurial likeability that makes us want to laugh at his jokes, score his goals, forgive his errors and support the causes he supports. Does it matter what is fact and what is myth? When all's said and done, we simply have to acknowledge Zlatan's status as one of the most complex, most original and above all most interesting characters in the game, someone who will certainly and deservedly be remembered as 'one of the greats'.

This is only a little book, but it is a tribute to the personality, humour and talent of a true giant. If in some small way it helps to cement Zlatan's incredible legacy – not that he needs that help – it will have served its purpose.

Zlatan, we salute you!

MALCOLM OLIVERS,
June 2017

1.
ZLATAN ON ...
ZLATAN

'Zlatan doesn't do auditions.'

Zlatan Ibrahimović

'When you buy me, you are
buying a Ferrari.'

Zlatan Ibrahimović

'The only time Zlatan was
wrong was when he thought
he had made a mistake.'

Zlatan Ibrahimović

'First I went left, and he did too. Then I went right, and he did too. Then I went left again, and he went to buy a hot dog.'

Zlatan Ibrahimović

'I can't help but laugh at
how perfect I am.'

Zlatan Ibrahimović

'Zlatan's computer has no
"backspace" button – Zlatan
doesn't make mistakes.'

Zlatan Ibrahimović

'My dog picks up its
own mess. Zlatan will not
take shit from anyone.'

Zlatan Ibrahimović

'One thing is for sure.
A World Cup without Zlatan
is nothing to watch.'

Zlatan Ibrahimović

'I think I'm like wine. The older
I get, the better I get.'

Zlatan Ibrahimović

'I don't like to talk
about myself.'

Zlatan Ibrahimović

2.
ZLATAN: MAN OR MYTH?

'Zlatan doesn't dial the wrong number – you pick up the wrong phone.'

Zlatan Ibrahimović

'Zlatan doesn't wear a watch.
He decides what time it is.'

Zlatan Ibrahimović

'Zlatan can make
scissors beat rock.'

Zlatan Ibrahimović

'Zlatan finished
The Neverending Story.'

Zlatan Ibrahimović

'Zlatan leaves messages
before the beep.'

Zlatan Ibrahimović

'When Zlatan does a push-up,
he isn't lifting himself up,
he's pushing the Earth down.'

Zlatan Ibrahimović

'Zlatan can light a
fire by rubbing two ice
cubes together.'

Zlatan Ibrahimović

'Zlatan counted to infinity.
Twice.'

Zlatan Ibrahimović

'Zlatan can slam a
revolving door.'

Zlatan Ibrahimović

'Zlatan is the greatest thing, period,
despite his invention of sliced bread.'

Zlatan Ibrahimović

'There is no theory of evolution,
just a list of creatures Zlatan
allows to live.'

Zlatan Ibrahimović

'When Zlatan was born, he
drove his mum home
from the hospital.'

Zlatan Ibrahimović

'... of course Zlatan can do
a wheelie. On a unicycle.'

Zlatan Ibrahimović

'Zlatan can kill two stones
with one bird.'

Zlatan Ibrahimović

'So maybe Jesus can walk
on water, but Zlatan can swim
through land.'

Zlatan Ibrahimović

'Zlatan once took a
lie-detector test. The machine
confessed to everything.'

Zlatan Ibrahimović

'When Mark Zuckerberg
invented Facebook, he already
had a friend request waiting
for him from Zlatan.'

Zlatan Ibrahimović

'Zlatan once won a game of
Russian Roulette with a
fully loaded gun.'

Zlatan Ibrahimović

'Zlatan can retweet a
Facebook post.'

Zlatan Ibrahimović

'Zlatan once had a staring
contest with the sun.
The sun blinked first.'

Zlatan Ibrahimović

3.
ZLATAN ON ...
ZLATAN

'One year ago today,
Zlatan announced the signing
of Manchester United.'

Zlatan Ibrahimović

'Zlatan doesn't tell lies.
He changes facts.'

Zlatan Ibrahimović

'What Carew does with a football,
Zlatan can do with an orange.'

Zlatan Ibrahimović

'An injured Zlatan is a pretty
serious thing for any team.'

Zlatan Ibrahimović

'Zlatan can play in all 11 positions.
A good player can play anywhere.'

Zlatan Ibrahimović

'Zlatan can hear sign language.'

Zlatan Ibrahimović

'When Zlatan plays darts,
he does an eight-dart
checkout, every time.'

Zlatan Ibrahimović

'When Zlatan plays snooker,
he always gets 148.'

Zlatan Ibrahimović

'Zlatan doesn't age.
He evolves.'

Zlatan Ibrahimović

'Zlatan once went for a
bike ride and accidentally
won the Tour de France.'

Zlatan Ibrahimović

4.
ZLATAN ON ...
ZLATAN AGAIN

'Only God knows . . .
You're talking to him now.'

Zlatan Ibrahimović

'At Barca, players were banned from driving their sports cars to training. I thought this was ridiculous – it was no one's business what car I drive – so in April, before a match with Almeria, I drove my Ferrari Enzo to work. It caused a scene.'

Zlatan Ibrahimović

'What every sports player should say after winning? "First of all, I would like to thank Zlatan for not competing."'

Zlatan Ibrahimović

'I didn't injure you on purpose, and
you know that. If you accuse me again
I'll break both your legs, and that time
it *will* be on purpose.'

Zlatan Ibrahimović

'Then Guardiola started his philosopher thing. I was barely listening. Why would I? It was advanced bullshit about blood, sweat and tears, that kind of stuff.'

Zlatan Ibrahimović

'We are looking for an apartment;
if we do not find anything, then
we will just buy a hotel.'

Zlatan Ibrahimović

'I came like a hero, left
like a legend.'

Zlatan Ibrahimović

'If I had played in England
I would have destroyed it, like
I have everywhere else.'

Zlatan Ibrahimović

'I think I am difficult to satisfy,
because when I win something,
I'm already thinking about the next
step, and that is maybe a problem
for me. I'm not enjoying the moment.
I'm already on the mission to
win the next trophy.'

Zlatan Ibrahimović

'Do you know what I love
about hunting? That I am no one
in the woods, no one at all. I thought
the animals might recognise me,
but they didn't. They did not even
ask me for any autographs.'

Zlatan Ibrahimović

5.

ZLATAN ON ...
ZLATAN

'If anything, the children of Paris
should be giving me even more money
for having the privilege of being in the
same city as my incredible quality.
And so should David Beckham.'

Zlatan Ibrahimović

'I do not need a trophy to tell
myself that I am the best.'

Zlatan Ibrahimović

'I have a big heart.'

Zlatan Ibrahimović

'Wherever I go, people recognise me,
call my name, cheer me.'

Zlatan Ibrahimović

'If I'd gone into taekwondo,
I'd probably have won several
Olympic medals.'

Zlatan Ibrahimović

'Some coaches prefer players who
will just do whatever he tells them to.
It's like, if you're at school with a load
of 10-year-old boys and you tell them
to jump, everyone will start to jump.
But the intelligent boy will ask,
"Why should I jump? Why?"'

Zlatan Ibrahimović

'Zlatan doesn't score lucky goals.
Goals are lucky to be scored
by Zlatan.'

Zlatan Ibrahimović

'How hard can it be to
learn Chinese?'

Zlatan Ibrahimović

'Zlatan's calendar goes straight
from March 31st to April 2nd.
No one fools Zlatan.'

Zlatan Ibrahimović

6.

ZLATAN ON ...
LIFE!

'When I took my shirt off against Caen, everybody asked what these new tattoos were. I had 15 removable tattoos on my body; they are the names of real people who are suffering from hunger in the world.'

Zlatan Ibrahimović

'I decide my future. I decide what I want to do. Nobody else. If I decide this will be my last year, maybe it is. If I decide it will be my last contract, I decide that. Nobody else. So I will decide when the moment is there.'

Zlatan Ibrahimović

'I had time with my mother, but
I really lived with my father. One time
he gave all his salary so I could travel
to a training camp. He couldn't pay
the rent, but he did that.'

Zlatan Ibrahimović

'The way that I opened the door for the young people that come from where I come from and that have a different background — that is what I want to be remembered for.'

Zlatan Ibrahimović

'Best player I ever played against?
I mean, I played against many, many
good players, so I don't know who to
keep. I would say Ronaldo the
Fenômeno.'

Zlatan Ibrahimović

'Nothing is written in stone,
as a career is an unpredictable
journey.'

Zlatan Ibrahimović

'Lionel Messi is awesome.'

Zlatan Ibrahimović

'I would love to play alongside
Wayne Rooney. He does the running
of two or three players and makes
a lot of space. We would be the
perfect combination.'

Zlatan Ibrahimović

'Anything that happens in your life was meant to happen. It is your destiny. I was destined to have the life I have now, and I can't have any regrets.'

Zlatan Ibrahimović

'I read all the time that people think I'm arrogant. They say I'm cocky, a bad character. I had that from a young age. But when they meet me, they say, "That image doesn't fit you."'

Zlatan Ibrahimović

7.
JOSÉ AND ZLATAN

'Ronaldo is a good player but he is certainly not the best. He deserved the Golden Ball award because his team won the Champions League and the Premier League. But, for me, Ibrahimović is the best.'

José Mourinho

'He was very angry and upset as he came at me. He was shouting, "We are champions, I helped a lot to make you champions, now nobody's helping me. I want to [come off] now."'

José Mourinho

'. . . but I pretended not to understand him. I said, "What? What? Do you want a drink, do you want some water?" and I threw him a bottle. I told him, "Here, take a drink and go." A few minutes later he scored a beautiful goal.'

José Mourinho

'A player who gave me as much as Ibra will always be in my heart. He did a lot for Inter and Inter did a lot for him. I like seeing Ibra. I greet him whenever I get the chance to and I wish him all the best – except when he plays against me. He is very special, he is one of the best strikers in the world.'

José Mourinho

'I don't understand when people say he is a difficult guy to work with or a difficult personality. When you have somebody that is a winner and wants to win all the time, I think he is very, very easy. I only coached him for a year but it was a good year, a good experience, and I rate him as one of the best players I have ever coached.'

José Mourinho

'José Mourinho is a big star. The first time he met my partner Helena, he whispered to her, "Helena, you have only one mission: feed Zlatan, let him sleep, keep him happy."'

Zlatan Ibrahimović

'That guy says whatever he wants.
I like him. He's the leader of his army.
But he cares, too. He would text me all
the time at Inter, wondering how I was
doing. He's the exact opposite of Pep
Guardiola. If Mourinho lights up a
room, Guardiola draws the curtains.
Mourinho would become a guy
I was basically willing to die for.'

Zlatan Ibrahimović

8.
OTHERS ON ...
ZLATAN

'He is a physically magnificent specimen ... I've played with or against the very best in the world. I want to say that I have never met anyone who was so serious during both practice and games. When I came to Paris I knew that he was an incomparable talent as a player, but he'd be so tough and merciless on himself at all times, I had no idea. He is a born winner. He is a beast with huge self-confidence, and I'm one of his biggest admirers.'

David Beckham

'Zlatan has always played at the top level. He never had a low point in his career. Perhaps he had some bad games now and then, but that's all. He has gained the respect of all his teammates and all his rivals. He is an example for every footballer.'

Eden Hazard

'We used to sleep in the same room before games. One night, he woke up. Ibra told me, "Adi, wake up! I had a nightmare. I dreamed Ronaldo was better than me!" He only went back to sleep after I told him, "No, Zlatan, no! You are the best in the world! Calm down!"'

Adrian Mutu

'The thing about Zlatan is this is a guy who always wants to win. Trust me, this guy would chase the last pass in the last minute of a training session in July if he thought he could get the goal that won the eight-a-side. When he says that he is getting better, he means it. He's certainly better than any 34-year-old footballer I know.'

Carlo Ancelotti

'He's someone who, as a player, you see him walk into the dressing room and you see a winner, you see a character and you're seeing a bit of class. As a teammate it lifts you. These are the signings that will lift the Manchester United team and that's what you want.'

Ryan Giggs

'He looks a good character. You'd be happy to play with him. As a player? Really, really good. Talented boy. Looks a bit of a character.'

Roy Keane

'He is an amazing player, someone really special who has marked an era. He has won league titles wherever he went. Of course, he can be quite temperamental. He says what he thinks, but that has never bothered me. There are not a lot of players with his character.'

Thierry Henry

'He is a world-class player and is a world-class person. Any team that gets him should be very grateful. He is fantastic – the way he speaks with the younger players, the way he demands quality. It is a true pleasure to play with him. There'll never be another Zlatan – he's a one-off. The way he talked and behaved has inspired me.'

John Guidetti

'I could see immediately that he had something special but I did not think he would become such a big star. He was big, good technically and could read the game. Zlatan is fantastic and, honestly, I get angry when people say bad things about him. He is an intelligent and pleasant guy. For me there are three players: Pelé, Johan Cruyff and Żlatan Ibrahimović. They are the three best players ever.'

John Steen Olsen (scout)

'[Zlatan] is a top-class player.
One of the best in Europe,
if not the world.'

Martin O'Neill

'It will be impossible to find another Zlatan. He is special, he is unique. We will not find another player like him in Sweden, because he is unique.'

Erik Hamrén

'It is difficult to defend against
him because he has the physique
of a big centre-forward, a "target man"
as we say here in English football.
But on top of that, he is technical
and quick like a small player. Few
players have both of those qualities,
so the defenders are not used to
that. You are pushed around, and
as well, you get out-dribbled
with finesse . . .'

Kurt Zouma

'He's a fit lad, he looks after himself, he's got great charisma. He's a great character.'

Paul Scholes

'Zlatan Ibrahimović has tremendous leadership qualities. He was the hardest I'd ever seen on his own team-mates about standards, whether the kind of ball [played], the effort, off-the-field stuff. That's a big part of why he's got to where he is. He's so arrogant he's actually likeable.'

Paul Clement

'This guy finds the goals, finds the little tricks. He finds whatever the crowd needs at any given time. He was born to play for Manchester United.'

Peter Schmeichel

'We haven't had a goalscorer like
him in France for a long time.
He is on a different planet to
anyone else.'

Jean-Pierre Papin

'Zlatan Ibrahimović is the
greatest foreign player ever
to play in France.'

Christophe Galtier

'He has a strong personality but people in front of their TV think that he is arrogant. He is not arrogant. He is still very good, and for PSG he is a very, very important player. I think he is one of the best players I played with. I played with Seedorf, Ronaldinho, Pirlo, Nesta — they are all quality players. He is different. He is strong physically and he also has technique, but he has a bigger personality. That makes him a great player.'

Thiago Silva

'He has an ego, but on the field he behaves like a champion. It's part of his character. No one will change his personality, like Cristiano Ronaldo. Sometimes he shows an arrogant side, but when you know him he's not like that at all. He's quite nice.'

Zinedine Zidane

'His statistics are unbelievable. He is an incredible competitor. He wants to win everything, he wants to score more goals. When I hear people questioning his abilities, it means they don't know a thing about football. He can have difficult patches of form, but when you see what he has done – and I don't think it's over – I think it's impressive.'

Laurent Blanc

'Zlatan is unique – he's the only
player in the world who measures 1.96
metres, has the technique of Lionel
Messi, the character of Muhammad Ali
and the strength of Mike Tyson.'

Mino Raiola

'When he's on form, he's unstoppable. He's at the same level as [Cristiano] Ronaldo and Messi. He has the strength, the technique and the intelligence. He's an extraordinary player.'

Gianfranco Zola

'I have played with Leo [Messi], Cristiano [Ronaldo], Rooney, and now I have the chance to play with Zlatan. I'd never realised how good he is, all the moves he has, despite him being so tall. I think he has a lot of quality.'

Ángel Di Maria

'Of course it will be hard for anybody to do what Van Basten did during his career ... the way he [Zlatan] moves with the ball really does remind me of Van Basten.'

Paolo Maldini

'Zlatan is a beast. He is one of those players that I like because of his character and his quality. He is among the best strikers in football history.'

Diego Costa

9.
SPECIAL ZLATAN BONUS WORD SEARCH

A	Z	A	T	A	Z	L	A	T	A	N	A
A	T	Z	A	Z	L	Z	Z	A	T	L	T
Z	Z	L	A	T	A	N	T	L	Z	A	Z
Z	L	A	T	A	T	A	N	Z	Z	A	L
A	A	T	A	N	A	Z	A	Z	L	T	A
L	T	N	Z	Z	N	A	Z	T	A	L	T
T	A	Z	L	T	A	T	L	A	N	Z	A
A	N	Z	A	Z	L	L	A	T	A	Z	N
Z	A	Z	T	A	Z	Z	T	A	L	Z	T
L	L	T	A	A	Z	L	A	T	A	N	A
A	Z	A	N	L	L	A	N	Z	T	Z	Z
T	A	N	L	Z	L	A	A	T	T	A	N

HONOURS

Individual*

Swedish Football Personality of the Year: 2002
Eurosport Goal of the Year: 2004 vs NAC Breda
UEFA Euro 2004 Man of the Match:
    Sweden vs Italy
Serie A Most Loved Player: 2005
Jerringpriset: 2007
Serie A Goal of the Year: 2008 vs Bologna
UEFA Euro 2008 Man of the Match:
    Sweden vs Greece
Ballon d'Or: 2005 (8th place), 2007 (7th place),
    2008 (9th place), 2009 (7th place)
Serie A Foreign Footballer of the Year (3): 2005,
    2008, 2009

* All statistics are from https://en.wikipedia.org/wiki/
Zlatan Ibrahimović

Serie A Footballer of the Year (3): 2008, 2009, 2011

2011 Supercoppa Italiana: Man of the Match

Serie A Team of the Year (2): 2010–11, 2011–12

Golden Foot: 2012

Serie A Top Scorer (2): 2009, 2012

UEFA Euro 2012 Man of the Match: Sweden vs France

UEFA Euro Team of the Tournament: 2012

UEFA Champions League Most Assists: 2012–13

FIFA Ballon D'Or: 2012 (10th place), 2013 (4th place)

FIFA FIFPro World XI: 2013

FIFA Puskás Award: 2013

Swedish Goal of the Year (2): 2012, 2013

UEFA Best Player in Europe Award: 2011 (8th place), 2013 (9th place)

UEFA Team of the Year (4): 2007, 2009, 2013, 2014

ESM Team of the Year (4): 2006–07, 2007–08, 2012–13, 2013–14

UEFA Champions League Team of the Season: 2013–14

2014 Trophée des Champions: Man of the Match

Ligue 1 Goal of the Year: 2014 vs Bastia

2015 Coupe de la Ligue Final: Man of the Match

Swedish Male Athlete of the Year (4): 2008, 2010, 2013, 2015

UEFA Ultimate Team of the Year (substitute; published 2015)

UNFP Player of the Month (6): September 2012, January 2014, February 2014, March 2014, November 2015, December 2015

Ligue 1 Player of the Year (3): 2012–13, 2013–14, 2015–16

Ligue 1 Team of the Year (4): 2012–13, 2013–14, 2014–15, 2015–16

Ligue 1 Top Goalscorer (3): 2012–13, 2013–14, 2015–16

Guldbollen (11): 2005, 2007, 2008, 2009, 2010, 2011, 2012, 2013, 2014, 2015, 2016

Eurosport European Player of the Month: August 2016

PFA Fans' Premier League Player of the Month: December 2016

Premier League Player of the Month: December 2016

Alan Hardaker Trophy: 2017

Swedish Forward of the Year (11): 2005, 2007, 2008, 2009, 2010, 2011, 2012, 2013, 2014, 2015, 2016

UEFA Europa League Squad of the Season: 2016–17

A.C. Milan Hall of Fame

Club

Ajax
Eredivisie: 2001–02, 2003–04
KNVB Cup: 2001–02
Johan Cruyff Shield: 2002

Internazionale
Serie A: 2006–07, 2007–08, 2008–09
Supercoppa Italiana: 2006, 2008

Barcelona
La Liga: 2009–10
Supercopa de España: 2009, 2010
UEFA Super Cup: 2009
FIFA Club World Cup: 2009

A.C. Milan
Serie A: 2010–11
Supercoppa Italiana: 2011

Paris Saint-Germain
Ligue 1: 2012–13, 2013–14, 2014–15, 2015–16
Coupe de France: 2014–15, 2015–16
Coupe de la Ligue: 2013–14, 2014–15, 2015–16
Trophée des Champions: 2013, 2014, 2015

Manchester United
FA Community Shield: 2016
EFL Cup: 2016–17
UEFA Europa League: 2016–17

OTHER
ACHIEVEMENTS

General

The only player to score in the UEFA
   Champions League for six different teams:
   Ajax, Juventus, Internazionale, Barcelona,
   A.C. Milan, Paris Saint-Germain

The only player to have won 13 championships
   in four different leagues: Eredivisie, Serie A,
   La Liga, Ligue 1

One of two players, along with Cristiano
   Ronaldo, to have scored a goal in every
   minute of a football match during their
   careers

One of two players, along with Ronaldinho, to
   have scored at least one goal in the *Derby
   della Madonnina* in Italy, *El Clásico* in Spain
   and *Le Classique* in France

The only foreign player to have won

Capocannoniere with two different teams, in addition to two teams from the same city: Internazionale (2008–09) and A.C. Milan (2011–12)

The only player to have scored at least one goal in *De Klassieker* in Netherlands, the *Derby della Madonnina* and *Derby d'Italia* in Italy, *El Clásico* and *Derbi barceloní* in Spain, *Le Classique* in France, the Manchester derby and North-West derby in England

Sweden

All-time top goalscorer for Sweden

Most Guldbollen: 11

Most consecutive Guldbollen: 10 (2007–16)

Sweden's top goalscorer in UEFA European Championship: 6 goals

Sweden's only player to score in three consecutive UEFA European Championship tournaments: 2004, 2008, 2012

Barcelona

The only player to score in his first five league
matches

Paris Saint-Germain

Top goalscorer in official competitions
Top goalscorer in Ligue 1
Only Paris Saint-Germain player to be top
goalscorer in three Ligue 1 seasons (2012–13,
2013–14, 2015–16)
Most Ligue 1 goals in a season: 38 in
2015–16
Fastest Ligue 1 hat-trick: 9 minutes (vs Troyes,
13 March 2016)
Longest goalscoring run in Ligue 1: 9 matches
in 2015–16 season (shared with Vahid
Halilhodžić)
Most goals scored in a single season: 50 in
2015–16

Paris Saint-Germain record goalscorer in UEFA
   competitions: 20 goals

Manchester United

The second player (after Ian Storey-Moore in
   1971–72 season) to score in his first three
   league matches
The second player (after Javier Hernández in
   2010–11 season) to score in the Premier
   League, FA Cup, League Cup, European
   competition and Community Shield in a
   single season (2016–17)
The fourth player to reach 15 goals in the lowest
   number of matches: 23 matches, behind
   Ruud van Nistelrooy (19 matches), Dwight
   Yorke (20 matches) and Robin van Persie
   (21 matches)

Premier League

Scorer of the 25,000th Premier League goal

The third player to have scored 14 goals in the first 20 Premier League games (shared with Alan Shearer and Sergio Agüero)

The oldest player to reach 15 goals in a single season (2016–17 season at 35 years and 125 days)

CAREER
STATISTICS

International

Appearances and goals for Sweden

Year	Apps	Goals
2001	5	1
2002	10	2
2003	4	3
2004	12	8
2005	5	4
2006	6	0
2007	7	0
2008	7	2
2009	6	2

Year	Apps	Goals
2010	4	3
2011	11	3
2012	8	11
2013	11	9
2014	5	3
2015	10	11
2016	5	0
Total	116	62

Club

As of matches played to 20 April 2017

Club	Years	Seasons	Apps	Goals
Malmö FF	1999-2001	3	47	18
Ajax	2001-05	4	110	48
Juventus	2004-06	2	92	26
Internazionale	2006-09	3	117	66
Barcelona*	2009-10	1	46	22
A.C. Milan*	2010-12	2	85	56
Paris Saint-Germain	2012-16	4	180	156
Manchester Utd	2016-17	1	46	28
Career total			**723**	**420**

* 2010-11: on loan from Barcelona to A.C. Milan.